Petals of the Heart

Swami Pranavamritananda Puri

Mata Amritanandamayi Center
San Ramon, California, USA

Petals of the Heart
Swami Pranavamritananda Puri

Published by:
    Mata Amritanandamayi Center
    P.O. Box 613
    San Ramon, CA 94583-0613, USA

Copyright © 2022 by Mata Amritanandamayi Center
All rights reserved.
No part of this publication may be stored in a retrieval system, transmitted, reproduced, transcribed or translated into any language in any form, by any means without the prior agreement and written permission of the publisher.

In India:
    www.amritapuri.org
    inform@amritapuri.org

In Europe:
    www.amma-europe.org

In US:
    www.amma.org

Dedication

*dhyāyāmaḥ suvibhātabhānuvadanām
sāndrāvabōdhātmikām
tattvajñānavibhūṣitāmabhayadām
tacchabdavidyōtikām
mandasmērasubhāṣitairnatikṛtām
sarvārtividdvamsikām
brahmānandaparāyaṇāmatulitā-
mambāmṛtākhyām parām*

We meditate on Amma, whose countenance is as radiant as the rising sun; who is pure consciousness embodied; who is adorned with the jewel of spiritual wisdom; who grants refuge to devotees; who kindles the knowledge of the Supreme in the hearts of disciples; who, with her sweet smile and ambrosial words, dispels the sorrows of the distressed; who is ever established in Brahman, the Supreme; who is peerless; and who has become renowned by the name Amrita.

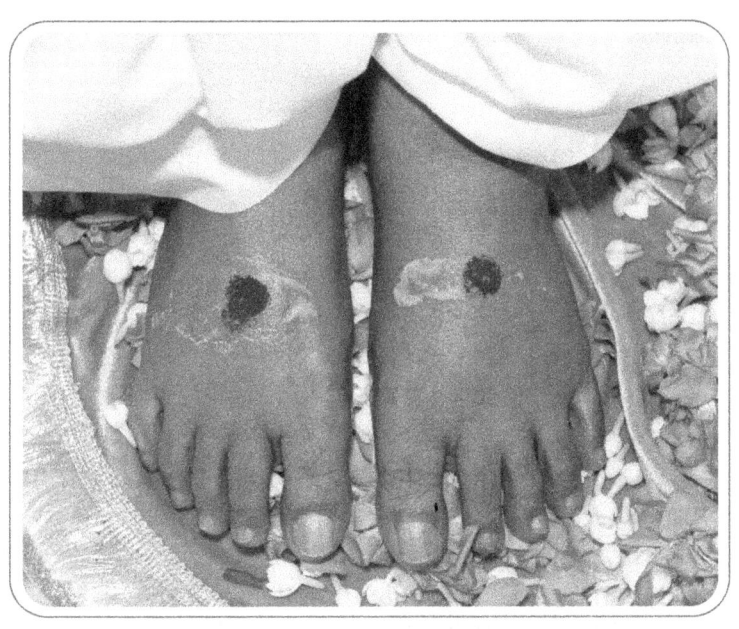

ōm amṛtāyai namaḥ

About the Author

Swami Pranavamritananda Puri joined the ashram in 1980 and is one of Amma's senior-most monastic disciples. He holds a B.Sc. degree in Zoology and an M.A. in Sanskrit Literature. In accordance with Amma's instructions, Swamiji has been teaching Sanskrit to the ashram residents. He is also a featured speaker on the Amrita TV channel.

A reputed singer and percussionist, Swamiji has accompanied Amma to various programs in India and abroad. He has written and scored many devotional songs. Swamiji is the author of *My Mother, My Master* (English), *Dawn of the Divine* (English), *Way of the Wise* (English), *Amma Nalkiya Pathangal* (Malayalam) and *Amrita Sougandhikam* (Malayalam). This is his sixth book.

Contents

The Master's Grace   11
Merging in God   19
Streak of White Light   23
Moving Ahead Carefully   29
Realize the Difference between Good and Evil   33
The Creator's Consummate Skills   41
Led Astray by Ego   47
As Long as I Live, So Long Shall I Learn.   51
An Ongoing Drama   57
Lament of the Jasmines   63
The Voice of Conscience   69
Countless Sea Waves   73
A Life that Spreads Fragrance   79
Bliss of Union   85

"Children, there will not be a trace of selfishness or anger in a Guru, who is a knower of the Self and who has risen above all likes and dislikes. A disciple who longs to attain spiritual liberation must have unshakeable faith in this. Only he who is so convinced will be able to see the Guru's rebukes as being for his own good. The attitude of a true disciple is marked by total, unconditional surrender. If he has such an attitude, he will become one with the Guru. Only one who is obedient to the Guru and has devotion to him will realize the Truth."

—Amma

The Master's Grace

It was the auspicious time of *Brahma-muhurta*,[1] when the seeker begins his daily spiritual practices and waits for the sun of knowledge to dawn and dispel the darkness of ignorance.

Every day, Aruna, the charioteer of the Sun-god, appears amidst a golden glow because he is carrying the idol of the sun. He does this daily in order to wake earthly beings from their nightly slumber.

Nikhil would start his daily spiritual practices well before the sun peeked above the horizon. He did so in the hope that his diligence would lead to the illumination of his soul.

Nikhil was different from the other disciples in the *Gurukula*.[2] While they dozed, oblivious to Lord Aruna's crossing, Nikhil would be awake even before his Guru arose. As Nikhil

---

[1] A period of time that begins one hour and 36 minutes before sunrise, and ends 48 minutes later. It is considered an auspicious time for all practices of yoga and most appropriate for meditation, worship or any other religious practice.
[2] Literally, the clan (*kula*) of the preceptor (*Guru*); traditional school where students would stay with the Guru for the entire duration of their scriptural studies.

was blessed with formidable dispassion, he could withstand all the coaxing from his mind to go back to bed.

After he finished his sadhana and greeted the rising sun, he would begin doing the duties his Guru had assigned him. He did them with utmost perfection and within the prescribed time. The other disciples, in contrast, were painfully slow to complete their tasks because they feared making mistakes and incurring the Guru's wrath.

Nikhil wanted to spend each and every moment in meditation. He did not want to waste a single second in his pursuit of the goal. As a consequence, he began to feel that worldly tasks hampered his spiritual growth. Nevertheless, when the Guru told him to clean the cowshed, sweep the monastery, or bathe the cows, he did so with total obedience.

Yet, Nikhil could not shake off the feeling that the tasks his Guru assigned him were inferior to the spiritual practice he so loved. Gradually, Nikhil began to do his seva hastily. This led to carelessness, which, in turn, led to broken pots, dirty kitchen utensils and unclean cows.

The Guru loved his disciple with all his heart though he had never been demonstrative in his affections. Pure love flowed silently as unseen grace upon Nikhil. Slowly, that gentle stream turned into a powerful tide. The Guru began to scold the disciple for doing work sloppily.

Nikhil became confused and, more than that, hurt. He had left family and friends, material wealth and even his clothes to be with the Master. He had shunned worldly life in the search for God. There had been no lapses in his *japa* (mantra chanting) or meditation. He had held his spiritual practices to the highest and strictest of standards. But because of his zeal for the goal, he did not realize that he had been doing his duties carelessly. As a result, his beloved Guru, who was his sole refuge, began chastising him daily for matters as insignificant as cleaning a cowshed.

After some time, Nikhil found these rebukes unbearable. The Guru did not seem to care who was around and punished him in front of the other students. Not only that, he began heaping love on them. He gave them priority and free rein to do as they pleased. He listened attentively whenever one of them came to speak to him on any matter. In any dispute between him and the other monks, the Guru accepted their words without question. Whenever the others proposed something, the Guru would implement it immediately, no matter how ill-conceived it seemed to be. The Guru even suggested that Nikhil look upon them as his role models!

Time in the Gurukula was to be spent in realizing God. Even if the others did not appreciate it, had his Guru forgotten it? Nikhil had once seemed to enjoy a special place in the Guru's heart, but the other students seemed to have usurped that place. The Master's words and actions were clear evidence that he no longer cared for Nikhil. Dejected, he began to feel that he would be better off somewhere else, a place dedicated to God-realization. Shouldn't diligence in meditation and prayer be a seeker's sole consideration? That being the case, how could one waste time on work?

With a heavy heart, Nikhil left the monastery early one morning. In spite of everything, he could not help but love his Guru, and it pained him intensely to leave him. He vowed to dedicate all his spiritual practices to his Guru, but he could not stay on in the monastery, which had become for him a place of darkness and distraction.

After wandering for some days, Nikhil reached the banks of a river. The sun's rays were glinting on the water ripples. He decided to take a dip in the cool waters. As he did so, his mind continued to prickle with thoughts of his Guru: Is Master sad that I'm not there? Is he trying to find me? Is he worried about me? He had no peace of mind but was determined not to succumb to the temptation of returning to the Gurukula.

The next morning, he woke up as usual during the Brahma-muhurta. As he began to meditate, he found that he could not think of anyone or anything except the Guru and the monastery. It was with this distracted mind that he later went to beg for alms. He was hungry as he had not eaten anything in the last few days.

After walking for some time, Nikhil spotted a house. As he approached it, he noticed an old man sitting in the courtyard and surrounded by children. He seemed to be teaching them. Drawing closer, Nikhil heard him say, "…you see, when the Master scolds someone, it is only because of love and because he wants the very best for the disciple. His anger is a mask. There is not even a trace of anger in his heart."

Nikhil began listening attentively. "The disciple won't know it, but the Guru will put him through tests and seemingly negative situations to eradicate his *vasanas* (latent tendencies). Often, the disciple does not use his faculty of discernment. The Guru is ever intent on making the disciple alert and on leading him forward to God. Only the Guru, who knows both the path and the goal, can give the precise instructions that the disciple needs to progress. The Guru's rebukes will always prove to be the disciple's saving grace. Actually, these rebukes are a form of compassion. The Guru will act in ways that are appropriate to the times. The disciple should see them as dharma made manifest, take refuge at his feet, and live with an attitude of surrender."

Hearing these words, Nikhil sat down abruptly; he could no longer remain standing under the burden of relief he felt at the old man's words. Had his Master been demonstrating pure love the whole time? He continued to listen as the wise man spoke.

"Only a true master can lead the disciple to the goal. At times, his tutelage may seem to take the form of stern criticism of the student's words and actions. But it is only out of true love that the Master takes a disciple to task; he does so only because he is interested in the disciple's highest good. To bring this about, the Guru will wear many masks, but he is motivated only by unconditional love and care. The disciple who is fortunate enough to hear even a harsh word from his master is blessed and must receive it as the Guru's *prasad*."[3]

When he had finished, the old man noticed Nikhil and gestured to him to come forward. "Here, young *sadhu* (monk), have some rice with my blessings."

With tears in his eyes and a heart full of longing for his Guru, Nikhil bowed to the old man and said, "Your words are the alms I needed. With your gift, I shall now return with great haste to my Guru's holy feet."

Nikhil scarcely felt heat or thirst, thorn or stone as he made his way home. He willed his feet to move faster and faster still so that he might kneel before his Guru.

When he finally reached home, he was drenched in perspiration. Nikhil fell prostrate at his Master's feet. The Guru embraced him and his eyes were glimmering with tears of affection. At that moment, Nikhil knew that he was where he ought to be. Beaming, the Guru said, "Child, you are not separate from me; we are one. Isn't it my duty to correct your mistakes? Not showing you too much affection and scolding you publicly—both are for your good. Do every action—and not just meditation, japa and other spiritual practices—with utmost alertness and awareness and without expectation of reward. Expectation often leads

---

[3] Consecrated offering.

to disappointment. If you can dedicate all your actions to God and work without expectation, you will be liberated once and for all from the grip of delusion. Equanimity and love will also dawn in your heart.

"In truth, only selfless actions qualify as karma yoga. Study Mother Nature, who is ever engaged in selfless service, and learn the lessons of altruism from her. Like the river, my grace and affection are constantly flowing towards you, but you are not aware of this, whereas I am. Child, if you can understand and control your own mind, you can understand everything."

Nikhil tearfully begged his Master, "O Guru, please forgive me for my rash behavior."

He prostrated again at the Guru's feet, silently praying that he never again becomes estranged from that sacred presence. Nikhil began to yearn to overcome the mountain of his ego and merge in the river of self-sacrifice and humility. Realizing that the Guru's words were sacrosanct, he decided to dedicate his life to the Guru.

Moral of the Story:

The grace and advice of a Guru, who is established in the highest truth, are indispensable to spiritual seekers. The Guru is a fount of wisdom. One who sees the Guru and God as different can never realize the Truth. But the one who realizes their oneness becomes the very embodiment of Om.

Amma says, "It is the mind that must be surrendered to God. Offering to him what the mind is attached to is akin to offering the mind itself. In truth, nothing belongs to us; everything belongs to God." ❈

"Children, the spiritual seeker need not try to gain anything, but only discard everything that is of no use. We must eliminate the ego. One who has not done so yet must constantly imagine oneself to be a mere instrument in the hands of the Guru."

—Amma

Merging in God

One day, Samved was playing in a field, admiring the pretty butterflies that flitted from one beautiful flower to another. When he returned home, a new object caught his eye—a pencil! At first, he did not think much about it but when he realized that it was from his uncle, who lived in the Middle East, he felt it was special.

The pencil's body was flexible and only as long as Samved's tiny hands. It was brightly colored. On one end was an eraser that looked like a hat.

Samved quickly forgot about the flowers and butterflies and spent all his time playing with the pencil. The pencil soon began to think that it occupied pride of place among Samved's playmates. It began to consider itself superior to everything and everyone else.

Samved was so enamored by the pencil that he began to play all kinds of pranks with it. He thought, "Why can't I brush my teeth with this pencil?" When he tried to do so, the pencil protested at being crushed against Samved's teeth. Thanks to the intervention of Samved's mother, the pencil was spared further discomfort. It noticed that Samved looked disappointed that its colors had not rubbed off on his teeth.

Merging in God

Next, Samved tried to use the pencil as a straw to drink milk. When he dipped the pencil in a glass of hot milk, the pencil started to cry in pain. But the hot milk was not moved or impressed by the pencil's cries. It made it clear that it did not want to have anything to do with the pencil.

As for Samved, he wasn't bothered by the pencil's cries, his mother's reprimands or the milk's protests. The pencil counted itself lucky to be alive and was desperate to escape his clutches. Though it could bend and twist into any shape, it could not stop Samved from continuing to use it anyway he liked.

Samved then started using the pencil to beat other boys. Seeing this, Samved's father decided, "This has gone too far." He decided to throw the pencil away. When he learned about the father's plan, Samved's uncle intervened. The pencil was relieved that it had not been consigned to the wastebin.

But its relief was short-lived. The uncle inserted the pencil into a sharpener and twisted it a couple of times. The pencil squirmed in pain as its outer sheath was shredded. He then used the pencil to draw a picture. Samved was amazed to see a picture emerge of baby Krishna. His uncle told him, "Color Krishna's body with the pencil. Be sure to stay within the lines, okay?"

Lying down on the floor, Samved happily colored the drawing with the pencil. Initially, the pencil sobbed at the thought that there was no end to its trials, as it was being rubbed against paper. After a while, it realized that it was merging with Krishna. After this, it did not cry when it was being sharpened, even though it hurt a great deal, because the pain was leading it to oneness with Krishna. It no longer mattered that its body was being sacrificed. After all, it was for a worthwhile purpose.

It is only when we shed our outer layers that we can discover our inner essence. It is in wearing away that we uncover our fullness. We will never be able to surrender if we cling to the ego. Realizing this, the pencil gradually became silent. Samved also understood that the pencil was merely an instrument for transferring his thoughts to paper.

Moral of the Story:

The misplaced pride of the pencil, which considered itself the owner's favorite, is the story of the ego. That pride led to sorrow. A Self-realized person realizes that he is only an instrument in the hands of God and rejoices in that. When we realize that we are also instruments in the hands of the Divine, it becomes easy to surrender. But this can happen only when we are ready to give up the ego. When we regard happiness and sorrow equally and consider them both fertilizers that can nourish our love for God, we will begin to appreciate the value of life. Only when we give up our own ideas of who we are, can we realize the true self. Just like the pencil's body is gradually worn away by the sharpener, spiritual practices will weaken our latent tendencies, allowing the mind to become as expansive as the blue sky and merge in God. It is only when we cease to identify with the body that we gain self-awareness. Merging in God is the highest fulfilment. ❈

"Selfish deeds might yield small pleasures. But if we work selflessly, the world will benefit in some way; we will also gain a measure of spiritual satisfaction. The fact is, it is the one who truly serves the world who becomes more refined and moves closer to perfection."

—Amma

Streak of White Light

We might amass wealth through relentless hard work, and then see ourselves flaunting it, the way a mountaineer proudly plants a flag on the summit after scaling the mountain.

But allowing greed to motivate our work is a waste of our energy. We don't always know what is best for us. The past, present, and future become confused in our minds—my wife (or husband), my home... We spend our days and nights building a nest on the frail twigs of the ego's dreams. It is only when we near our mortal end that we review the pages of our life and notice in each one the discernment that we lacked all along.

Curled up in a dark corner of an old-age home, Abhijit was sobbing silently. Once the titan of a vast business empire, he had since become destitute and wheelchair-bound. It was as if someone had sucked out all his energy. He thought, "Time mocks and terrorizes me by letting me linger here, taunting me like a devil. Time is a universal phenomenon and holds no man above the other. It stands witness as each of us cries in joy and in sorrow."

Though he did not realize it, a vital life-force was still thumping weakly within him. Feeling as if he were suffocating, he

moved to the small window in his room and with great difficulty pushed it open. Cool air caressed his face and a warm light shone upon his ragged countenance. The brilliance of the sun was shocking. He could see the sunshine even with eyes closed. Abhijit was used to a drab dimness. Having grown accustomed to the gloom, he was jolted by the prismatic rainbow of colors shining upon him through the window. Just as he was about to close the window, he saw Jitendran sitting under the banyan tree in the courtyard.

Abhijit had often tried to ignore Jitendran's smile, captivating though it was. He did not know why it was so attractive. It was as if a divine message of peace were emanating from those shining eyes. He wanted so much to be seated next to Jitendran so that he could unburden his mind. But he was unable to do so, possibly because of pride and an inferiority complex.

Abhijit recalled that he had always mocked monks. He had thought, "What's the purpose of life? Isn't it to enjoy ourselves?" Abhijit used to think that renunciates were dimwits to give up the pleasures of life.

But since then, renunciates like Jitendran had become the soul refuge for pleasure seekers like Abhijit, who had tired himself out in the playground of commerce. One can breathe a sigh of relief only when one has dropped all burdens at the feet of these spiritually illumined souls.

The spark in Jitendran's eyes and the peace that shone brightly forced Abhijit to think differently. He realized that only one who leads a life of non-possessiveness could show others the path of peace.

Abhijit thought, "Who wasted time in the past, Jitendran or I?" It was a good question to ask when you haven't recovered from the pitfalls of life. "I've never known the bliss that fills Jitendran. My life was governed by a desire to conquer everything while trying to protect my assets and double what I had gained. But all that I have to show for my pains are pain and sorrow. Perhaps, I might have enjoyed momentary pleasures from indulgence occasionally. Time passed. I still don't know what's true and what's untrue. Today, because my heart feels hurt and my body is wracked by pain, I feel like calling out to God.

"If only I had called out to God like this previously, I wouldn't be in this situation. Only if I had been wholly focused on God, the Lord's name would have ever remained on the tip of my tongue.

"Alas, I was trapped by the whirlpool of desire. Obsessed about the past and future, I had forgotten to live. I don't have much time left. The sands in the hourglass of life are trickling away. There is no point in chewing the cud of the past now. How can I become like an incense stick that exudes a sweet fragrance instead of being like a stinking trashcan? The past is over. I want to enjoy some peace in the remaining days of my life."

While Abhijit was thus ruminating, he felt the touch of a cool hand on his shoulder. Looking up, he saw that it was Jitendran. Unbelievable! They had never met like this before.

Jitendran said, "Don't allow yourself to get demoralized by fretting over your past deeds. Bid farewell to despair and regret, and welcome a new dawn of righteous living. It's possible, you know. God has said so and will stand by it; I'm sure of this."

Jitendran's words were like a gentle shower of peace. As the floodgates of his heart opened, Abhijit began to shed tears. He clung to Jitendran, like a creeping vine that grasps a great tree. Jitendran embraced Abhijit and caressed his head soothingly. Abhijit's whimpering was like that of an innocent child longing for its mother. Between sobs, he asked Jitendran, "Would you please help me and shed some light on the path of peace you walk? I've long lost my way and have stumbled along in darkness."

Jitendran took Abhijit's shivering hand in his and slowly began to lead him out of the jungle of darkness and along the path to eternal peace.

Moral of the Story:

What is the point of amassing wealth if we don't have peace of mind? If we have peace of mind, then the presence or absence of wealth will make no difference. It's hard to make the mind quiet. When we ruminate over the past or fantasize about wealth in the future, we miss the treasure in the present moment. We must learn from the past, dig deep into the present, and take peeks into the future. Once we stop lugging around the baggage of the past, we can walk freely in the present moment, offering our hands in service and devotion.

Amma says that the most important thing in spiritual life is *shraddha*—having faith in the words of the Guru and obeying them. There is nothing in the world that we can brush aside as insignificant. God is all-pervading, and hence, everything is imbued with the presence of the Divine. Only one who does every action, whether big or small, with shraddha and discernment can realize the Self. ❁

"Children often study well when they are young because of fear of punishment from the teacher. This fear helps them overcome laziness and acquire knowledge. By the time they reach the higher grades, they are no longer dogged by such fear as they would have gained the necessary discernment by then. They will have only reverence and obedience to the teacher. Most devotees have such an attitude towards God."

—Amma

Moving Ahead Carefully

Why was Ramnath like that? The word 'attentiveness' did not seem to exist in his dictionary. He was not serious about anything and did not pay attention to anything that anyone said, even after getting into so much trouble. One could only wonder how long it would take him to change.

Ramnath would let his concentration drift, like a dry leaf blown about by the breeze. His peers and others started ridiculing him for his lack of awareness.

Ramnath's Guru, who saw that his disciple was not making any progress, resolved to inculcate awareness in him through a bitter experience, which is the best teacher. By the power of his resolve, the Guru planted the seed of mischief in the minds of the other disciples.

One day, when he left the hermitage for a while, the other disciples decided to play a prank on Ramnath. They decided to exploit his inattentiveness. After some plotting, they went looking for Ramnath. When they saw him, one of them casually said, "You've been asked to go and get 'aravam'."

Moving Ahead Carefully

Hearing this, Ramnath left for the market without asking what it was, who wanted it, or why it was needed. When he reached the market, he entered the first store he saw and asked for aravam. Staring at the boy in disbelief, the owner muttered, "Such arrogance at this age!"

Ramnath went to another store and asked for the same thing. The proprietor sarcastically said, "I'll give you a few gooseberries. Grind them and apply the paste on your head to cool your brain down!"

Ramnath went to a third shop. When he asked for aravam, the store owner sternly asked him if he was trying to be funny.

Finally, owing purely to the Guru's grace, an old storekeeper who had overheard Ramnath's request asked him, "Child, do you know what you're saying? Aravam means 'loud noise.' Is that something you can buy?"

When he heard this, Ramnath was so embarrassed that he wanted to hide himself.

The storekeeper's words had awakened Ramnath's awareness, which was lying dormant. The boy understood what his fellow disciples had done. "What a fool I am!" he thought.

"Actions and words that lack discernment and awareness are unrighteous." Ramnath recalled these words of his Guru, and they reverberated deep within. He realized that only one in whom the light of awareness shines brightly can behold the Truth.

When he returned to the hermitage, he was received by the other disciples, who were laughing uncontrollably. Ramnath did not react. He thought, "Let them laugh. Who wouldn't laugh at a fool like me?"

He walked to his Guru's hut and saw him seated inside, radiating compassion. With a cry, Ramnath fell at the Guru's feet. Ramnath said, "If only I had paid attention to your words,

I would not have made such a fool of myself. Your divine play has opened my eyes."

The Guru said, "Son, don't despair. Don't think that you're the only one who is foolish. In a sense, isn't everyone ignorant? We must try to be mindful when we think, talk and act. Only one who is aware can succeed in spirituality or worldly life. The secret to success lies in clarity of thought. We must act with awareness and with a mind that is not clouded by too many thoughts."

Moral of the Story:

An inner awakening dawns only when we do even small actions with utmost care and alertness. The Upanishads and *Bhagavad Gita* emphasize this.

True alertness and awareness arise when we pay attention to the words of the Guru and strive to attain the Truth with an attitude of complete surrender. In order to realize the Truth, we need to have awareness, which is the essence of spirituality. Only one who realizes the eternal soul or the Self is truly aware.

One who knows his Self truly knows himself. Such a person has shraddha. Merely hearing the words of the Guru is not enough. We must listen with utmost attention so that we can understand and assimilate the sacred teachings. We must also practice them. This is the duty of the disciple.

In spiritual life, merely listening does not constitute *shravana*. Shravana refers to listening with faith and attentiveness. ❈

"Rare are those who do only good. Likewise, there will not be anyone who does only wrong. We must cultivate an understanding of what is wrong and the willingness to correct ourselves. If we can do that, God Himself will lead us by the hand to the Truth."

—Amma

Realize the Difference between Good and Evil

As soon as the monsoon rains started falling like divine grace on the scorched surface of the earth, winged ants, which have short lifespans, made their appearance. Before the monsoon, they can usually be seen on the trunks of trees. During the rainy season, one often feels hungrier. It is so with these winged creatures, too, who fly in search of food. To ensure that they would never be hungry during the monsoon, these ants decided to nest on the limb of a sprawling mango tree at the Mambilly ancestral home. The tree was festooned with fruits oozing sweet nectar. Though old enough to be a grandfather, the mango tree was standing erect like a sixteen-year-old, showing no signs of aging. It adorned the garden of the home and its canopy of leaves cast a cool shade. At least seven or eight generations from the Mambilly home have tasted the delectable fruits produced by this venerable mango tree.

That was when a winged ant noticed the crowds converging on the ancestral home. What was going on? The boughs of the mango tree seemed to be drooping under the weight of sorrow. There was a man digging deep in the shade of the tree. Feeling an ominous sense of foreboding, the winged ant shuddered.

Difference Between Good and Evil

That is when it heard the deep yet silent voice of the tree: "The youngest boy of the family met with a road accident and died."

"That trendy youth?" the ant asked in disbelief.

As the coffin was lowered into the grave, the crowd murmured in disbelief that death had snatched someone away in the prime of his youth. "Can't believe he's no more!"

The ant looked around. The birds had stopped twittering. Even the leaves were still. A mournful silence pervaded the air.

Unable to curb its sorrow, the mango tree began to sob. "Lay your head in my lap, dear son!" it rumbled.

Hearing the broken voice of the tree, the ant was moved to tears. Who would have thought the boy's lifespan would be as short as its own!

He had met with the accident while driving under the influence of alcohol. The mango tree spoke with paternal solicitude as it recalled events from the past. It said, "Every child born in this house has climbed up my limbs. This boy was mischievous: he would swing from my branches and pluck my fruits and flowers. But as he grew older, harmful desires darkened his heart. They were like parasites sucking his energy from within. After dusk, he and his friends would sit on my branches and smoke. The toxic vapor they exhaled would pollute the air. Unknown to his family members, the boy also became addicted to alcohol. However, as I am unable to voice my objections in a way that they can hear them, I could do nothing but bear the pain silently.

"On various occasions, when his parents told him off for loitering with his friends instead of praying at dusk, he would ridicule them: 'Chanting the names of God and thinking about Him are for oldies like you, who are in the twilight of their lives. How can you even ask someone like me to pray or chant divine names? Don't embarrass me in front of my friends. They will make fun of me and call me an old man!'

"Usually, people think of God in their final days because they fear death. But did this boy ever try to invoke the presence of the Divine? He did. When he was younger, I used to hear him pray loudly, 'O Lord, I beg you with all my heart. Hear my call! Protect the innocent!' How could he forget such prayers so quickly?

"A blade of grass cannot move without God's consent. Even our next breath is not in our hands. Knowing this, how can we live without thinking of God? Won't the awareness of God's presence make us humble and grateful and increase our self-confidence?"

So saying, the tree fell silent. To console it, the winged ant gently rubbed its legs on one of its branches.

The boy's father was still sitting under the mango tree and sobbing with grief. His tears fell to the ground that was already soaked by rain. Even nature seemed to be crying.

It was then that the ant noticed a group of young men walking towards the father. They were the close companions of the boy who had died. They were still reeling from the shock of losing their best friend and, at the same time, racked by guilt over what had happened. They approached the father with trepidation. When he looked up, the young men saw that the father's eyes were filled with sadness and anger. Unable to bear the looks of accusation, the men looked away. In those moments, they understood the full impact of what had happened and realized that nothing they did could ever undo the tragedy. They fell prostrate before the father and cried unabashedly.

The father saw his son's face in each one of them. An intense rage began to burn in his heart. He asked, "You went to the bar under the pretext of studying together. What did you gain? Are you satisfied now?"

His words, laced with bitterness, made the men feel even more remorseful. One of them tearfully said, "What we did is unpardonable. We never imagined that such a mishap would occur. Please do not curse or hate us. Please forgive us!"

Hearing this response, the father sobbed inconsolably. With his son's death, all his expectations as a father had been dashed. After some time, his sobs subsided. In an abstracted mood, he mumbled to himself, "If he had used his time properly, this accident would never have happened. Often, he would come home late at night and continue sleeping well after sunrise. His excuse was that he was tired after studying with his friends the whole night. But what's the use of brooding over all this now?"

After moments of silence, the father started mumbling again. "How many times did I object to the company he was keeping? I only did so because I had suspicions of their wayward character. But every time I spoke up, my son would get offended and we would quarrel. He would justify his actions. I advised him several times to come home before dusk so that we could pray together. Whenever I said that, he would mock me, saying that prayers are not for the young.

"I could only pray to God to forgive him for his immaturity and to lead him along the right path. Alas, my darling son is no more. Time did not wait for him. O Lord, may his soul have merged in you!"

Hearing his piteous words, the friends were at a loss for what to do or say. They felt suffocated by guilt. They knew that nothing they said or did could heal the father's broken heart. His lamentations made them realize anew how they had been opposing and deceiving their own parents. They felt that they could never atone for their sins sufficiently. One of them cried, "O God, why did you spare us? You should have taken our lives also in the accident!"

Hearing these words, the father looked up. He said, "You have squandered your life until now. What are you going to do next? Why don't you pray to God with an aching heart to lead you along the right path? No other father should undergo the tragedy that I am experiencing."

As if endorsing the father's words, the mango tree began to shake its leaves. The tree rumbled, "On several occasions, when these boys were dozing off in my shade under the influence of alcohol, I'd warned them, 'It's alright to enjoy yourself but never allow worldly pleasures to consume you. This rare and precious human birth is not to be wasted on material pleasures but to be spent on realizing God.' But they did not pay heed to my words, even though I advised them several times."

The ant reminded the mango tree, "I don't think they understand our language. They cannot hear us."

Ignoring the ant, the tree rumbled again. "God gave them an exalted human life to realize the Self, not to indulge in a life of forgetfulness by eating, drinking and making merry. But these boys do not realize this.

"Anyway, everyone must pay for their mistakes. We might be able to deceive the world, but who can deceive the Lord, the omniscient one? One needs to cultivate reverence towards God from childhood.

"These youngsters used to say that they would resort to prayer in their old age. A person who thinks like that is like a fool who looks for dry firewood during the rainy season. May the Almighty knock some sense into these youngsters."

Slowly, an air of peace began to spread all around, as if the words of wisdom uttered by the mango tree had been absorbed by the atmosphere.

One of the young men stood up, walked over to the father, sat down next to him, and said, "Father, we pledge never to hurt anyone ever again by word or deed. We swear to give up our vices." He then took the father's hand and, placing his own

Difference Between Good and Evil

on it, said, "Your son will live through us. We will fulfill all the wishes you had for him."

Something stirred in his father's heart. For the first time since his son's death, the father felt a sense of hope.

The man who had spoken then stood up and invited the others to do so. They stood by the freshly dug grave and repeated these words: "We will never again do anything that will hurt our families or society. Instead of being a slave to desires, we will work for the benefit of others."

After a pause, the young man said, "Dear friend, your departure is an irrecoverable loss. Nevertheless, we will serve your father as his children. May your soul find peace."

The father prayed, "O Lord, lead them along the path of love and compassion."

As the rains continued to pour, the father walked away with the young men on either side. The winged ant and the mango tree gazed at them and silently prayed that they redeem all the lost opportunities and make the best of life.

Moral of the Story:

It is good to repent for one's mistake, but it is better not to make the mistake in the first place. Fear of death is of no help to anyone, but an awareness of mortality helps us live righteously. Amma says that death is the greatest Guru. ⚘

"Children, God dwells in the heart of every being. Divine consciousness pulsates in everyone. For God, who is all-pervading, the acts of creation, sustenance and dissolution are mere lilas, a divine play. Beholding His sublime glory in everything will help us get rid of our ego. One who realizes the infinitude of God becomes one with Him."

—Amma

The Creator's Consummate Skills

Unni's tiny little eyes opened like two buds. It was not his mother who woke him up today but the gentle breeze laden with the fragrance of flowers. What was the first thing he saw? The auspicious form of Lord Krishna. As soon as he finished praying before the idol of the Lord, Unni dashed out of the house. The garden was redolent with the sweet scent of jasmines. "I shall pluck them all today," thought Unni. The next moment, he thought, "No! I must not do that."

Unni's father was deeply engrossed in reading the newspaper. To get his attention, Unni said, "Father, it was the scent of the flowers that woke me up today. What a pleasure it is to wake up to such a wonderful fragrance. I won't pluck any flowers today!"

Unni's father was impressed by his son's words. "To say such a wise thing, you must have been touched by divine grace. We can avail ourselves of God's grace only if we love everything. Unni, why can't you shower your affection all the time on the flowers, butterflies and the gentle breeze laden with the perfume of flowers?"

His father's comment gave Unni pause. He thought, "I love my parents. Isn't that enough? Why should I love everyone and everything else also?"

The father tried to open up the expansive world of pure love to his son. "Unni, flowers, butterflies, little birds, the breeze and everything else in this world are creations of God. Hence, you must love them all equally."

Hearing this, Unni thought, "Is Father saying all this only to prevent me from doing any mischief? How does he know that God exists? After all, we haven't seen God face to face."

As if responding to Unni's thoughts, his father said, "Don't we need strength to say 'I am weak'? Similarly, even the faculty of doubting (if God exists) depends on our having consciousness, which is nothing but God."

Unni's father continued. "Suppose I told you that Mother did not make *idlis* and curry today for breakfast; they appeared automatically. The plates, table and chairs also came into being by themselves, as did this house. Would you believe me?"

Unni's burst out laughing, as if he had just heard something hilarious. The laughter began to subside when his father asked, "Why are you laughing? Son, if all these things cannot manifest by themselves, how can this universe come into being on its own?

"The cashew tree that Unni climbs to pluck the fruit, its fragrance, the scores of mangoes on the mango tree in the front yard, the birds that come in search of them, the constellation of stars that glitter in the darkness, the moon that waxes and wanes... Who created all these?

"Who imbued the sun, which is the source of light, with so much energy? What power sustains the earth, ocean, fire, wind and sky? By whose command do the planets circumambulate

the sun along a fixed route? What prevents these huge planets from colliding? Who dictates the laws of the universe?

"Who is behind the perennial rotation of Mother Earth that divides a day into night, for us to sleep, and morning, for us to be awake? Who nourishes the billions of living beings on this vast earth with sunlight, fresh air, water and food?

"There is so much more to this universe than meets the eye. How can we say that there is no creator behind this bewildering variety? Wouldn't that be utterly foolish?"

Hearing his father's description of the universe, Unni's mind began to reel. His father gazed at his son affectionately and said, "Do you think this universe, with its hills and valleys, winds and rains, flowers and fruits, birds and beasts, oceans and rivers, and human beings, can automatically come into existence? How can we say that there is no power behind this?

"God is the one who creates, sustains and destroys the universe. But it's not possible to see the omnipotent God with our naked eyes. However, we can behold Him with our inner eye if we purify our mind through the chanting of divine names and meditation. Unni, if you want to see God, pray sincerely every day and try to make your mind one-pointed. True success in life is not about gaining a higher education and getting a well-paid job. It is attaining God."

When Unni heard this, his eyes lit up. He went to bathe and then ran to the puja room to pray.

Moral of the Story:

A pot implies the handiwork of a potter. Similarly, if there is a universe, there must be a lord of the universe. To say, "There is no God," there must be an 'I' present. In fact, there must be an 'I' even to say, "I do not exist." If we inquire, "Who am I?" we will realize that 'I' is God. To realize God, who is omnipresent and immutable, we must open our heart and turn inward. ❀

"Desires beget sorrow. Even though we know that expectation brings disappointment in its wake, we still continue to expect. What else is this but Maya? Children, ignorance is nothing but body consciousness. Only if we get rid of our ego and realize that this personality, which we associate with the body, is nothing can we become one with the all-pervading consciousness. Death will snatch away every thing we have gained in life. Hence, there is no reason to become egoistic."

—Amma

Led Astray by Ego

This story has two main characters: Meenambari and Keshav. Both are associated with the Meenagandhika backwaters. Meenambari remains under water, and Keshav, on the surface of it.

Meenambari would boast, "I'm the most beautiful fish in the Meenagandhika."

Hearing this, the others would mutter, "What a vain-pot!"

Dismissing such comments as jealousy, Meenambari would think, "Let them say what they want. Is there any fish here who doesn't envy my shining scales? I've even seen those humans with nets eyeing me with keen interest. But their tricks won't work with me, for I can swim away swiftly. I'm a big-time golden fish. I like things that glitter. When I see the golden stars twinkling in the sky, I try to leap high. Whenever I rise above the water surface, the river pulls me down. But one day, I shall escape these backwaters and attain the realm of the stars. That is when these fish will realize that I am a Goddess!"

Meenambari would fantasize about sprouting golden wings, soaring to the sky, and gliding there, a glamorous star among stars! While thus dreaming, Meenambari's mouth would be half open. Her eyes would glow with expectation. She spent her days and nights lost in reverie.

Once, during a moonless night, the fishermen lit a lantern to navigate their way through the waters. At the helm of the boat was Keshav, who knew how to gauge the depths of Meenagandhika. The splashing of the oars and the loud talk of the other fishermen drowned out the wind's humming of the *Omkara*—the 'OM' sound.

Suddenly, there was a thud. The fishermen were startled. Keshav raised the lantern to look at what had fallen into the boat. He smiled and said, "It's a golden fish!"

"Very good! Tonight's dinner is taken care of," said one of the fishermen. Keshav then told them, "It's hard to remove the scales of this fish. But we can still make a delicious curry by scoring lines deep in its flesh." Hearing this, the fishermen's mouths started salivating in anticipation.

While leaping out of the water, Meenambari had fallen into the boat and hit her head hard on the floor of the boat. As she lay there, writhing and gasping for breath, she heard the fisherman talking about gouging her flesh. "I hope I die before that!"

Meenambari had been fooled by the light from the lantern, mistaking it for a star. She recalled her grandmother's words: "Not all that glitters is gold."

As she lay dying, Meenambari reflected on her follies. "I thought fulfilling desires was the goal of life. Mistaking the lantern for a shining star, I leapt to my death. Now, my shimmering scales, which I flaunted throughout my life, have no value. I frittered away my whole life in fairy-tale fantasies. Instead of swimming towards the infinite ocean of spiritual bliss, I splashed around in the backwaters of egocentric thoughts. I failed to realize that the glamour of self-centeredness is fake and could not perceive the subtle light of pure knowledge. O

Lord, my life is now going to end ignominiously on the dinner table of cruel men!"

By God's grace, in the final moments of her life, Meenambari was able to discriminate between the eternal and the ephemeral. Just before Keshav plunged the knife into her, true knowledge dawned in her heart.

Moral of the Story:

Being bound by 'lust and gold' throughout life is a deplorable waste of time. The attachments that arise from desire invariably lead us down the path of ignorance and delusion. Whereas attachment to the body keeps us trapped in materialism, Self-realization helps us rise to the realm of the divine.

'Asha hi paramam duhkham'—'Desires are the main cause of sorrow.' Let us strive to cleanse our minds of excessive desire or greed, and thus, move towards bliss, which is our true nature.

"Children, nature is nothing but our mind. That is why Amma tells you to study nature. Mother Nature is always teaching us the lessons of love, renunciation and surrender. One who observes nature carefully will gain the inspiration to introspect and purify the mind. Therefore, Mother Nature is both scripture and Guru. Children, learn lessons from nature and cultivate inner refinement and purity."

—Amma

As Long as I Live, So Long Shall I Learn.

The shadows of the trees were playing hide and seek with the rays of the early morning sun. The mud trail parallel to the trees stretched for 16 kilometers. Thereafter, it started to meander. On the other side of the path lay paddy fields. Adorned by water droplets, the fields looked like a gem-studded, emerald sari. The scene was so captivating that one wonders if Beauty had chosen to isolate herself here.

The charms of flora and fauna can arrest the wandering mind and lead it towards inner bliss. There are numerous lessons to be learnt from the book of nature—from mountains, oceans, rocks, birds, forests and rivers. If we watch carefully, we can see much. And if we listen carefully, we can hear stories of self-sacrifice and surrender.

The broken rocks from the mountain eventually become stones. Some of these stones end up in rivers, which wend their way to the ocean. The unrelenting flow of the rivers polish and smooth the rough edges of some stones; the other stones are transformed into crystals of sand with which children play.

As Long as I Live, So Long Shall I Learn.

These are just some of the stories of the stones. Imagine how many other stories the forests, mountains and other beings in nature have to tell.

The early morning walk that my son and I took to the *mana*[4] was rejuvenating to the eyes and mind. We felt an indescribable inner satisfaction. We had embarked on this venture at the insistence of our Sanskrit Master. He had once said, "The foundation of this land of the *rishis* (seers) are the Vedas. The Vedas are our mother. Shouldn't children know their mother tongue? Shouldn't all of us learn at least a little Sanskrit, the language of the Vedas? The extinction of the language will lead to an extinction of our culture. Therefore, it is imperative that we study Sanskrit.

"For as long as we live, we should learn. There are no age restrictions in education and no end to learning. Life is a series of experiences, which are guides. Every experience is a teacher."

And so it was that we set out on a journey to learn the Vedic language. Walking along the ridges of the paddy fields in the wee hours of the morning, I felt I was regaining my youth. My son said that his heart was overflowing with joy. As we walked, we took in the sights around us—green grass and leaves, birds and animals... Equally, we were anticipating the sacred language awaiting us at the end of our blessed journey. Every week, we would look forward eagerly to these weekend jaunts.

Though the ridges were slushy after the rains, we reached the gates of the home without slipping. No one seemed to be home. The porch was littered with fallen leaves, mud and rainwater. Clearly, no one had swept the place in days.

Hearing our voices, an elderly woman emerged from the house. She wiped the perspiration from her forehead, laid the broom aside, washed her hands, and deferentially joined her

---

[4] The traditional homes of Brahmins in Kerala.

palms together in greeting. She said, "We were away for the last four or five days and just returned early this morning. After seeing the state of the porch, I decided to do some cleaning before starting any other work. I was sweeping the eastern side just now. Please come in and take a seat. Your teacher will come down any moment now."

The rainclouds had dispersed. The dewdrops on the grass were glistening in the morning sun, which had cast a gentle shadow on earth. The elderly woman seemed to be sketching a picture on the ground as she raked the leaves away.

My son asked, "Father, the porch is routinely swept every day. And yet, within just four days, it became so dirty."

Before I could say anything, we heard the voice of the Sanskrit teacher. "Son, you're right. If we don't sweep the grounds daily, they will become dirty. The human mind is no different. If we don't focus on the Almighty, the mind will become a breeding ground for separation and egoism. The juggernaut of time will crush the life that is riddled with desires. Only those who are self-sacrificing can rise above time.

"Though we know what's right and what's wrong, goaded by desire, many of us still run after the wrong. If a polluted mind is like a dark night, a pure mind steeped in culture and tradition is like a resplendent morning."

Leading them to the living room, the teacher continued. "Don't think of Sanskrit as just a language. Those who want to uplift themselves or steep the mind in the Indian culture and tradition must study Sanskrit, which is a vehicle for our tradition or culture. If we do so, we can sweeten our lives with lofty wisdom."

After this introduction, my son and I began learning Sanskrit and absorbing many lessons.

Moral of the Story:

Just as the grounds, which had not been cleaned for four days, became cluttered with leaves and mud washed away by the rain, a mind that has not engaged in Self-inquiry becomes tainted by desires, arrogance and attachments. But a mind that contemplates daily on spiritual principles gradually becomes purified and divinized through meditation. Learning Sanskrit, which is a portal to the scriptures, plays a major role in making the mind purer and more expansive.

Whereas ignorance drags one into the cesspool of filth, spiritual knowledge is like the steps leading to the sanctum sanctorum, where God is enshrined.

Learning does not stop at any age. Knowledge is of no use if it is not practical. True education is self-analysis. The wise men and women who show us the path to Self-realization have self-awareness and are spiritually illumined. ❀

"Our actions ought to broaden our minds and make our hearts more expansive. If we have this attitude, every deed we do will be sincere. If we constantly bear in mind that God is watching our every move, we will act carefully. Karma-phala, or the fruits of our actions, is like a constant and inseparable companion. No other gain in life will accompany us hereafter; only our karma-phala. It will be with us in birth, life and death. Children, we must live in the world with the awareness that only God is eternal."

—Amma

An Ongoing Drama

If you had witnessed the fights between Amal and Kalyani, you would have wondered what the problem was between them. Both are like tigers that have lost their teeth. Though their hair is whiter than snow and their skin, more wrinkled than crumpled clothes, old age has not lessened the intensity of their conflicts. Such was the contentious nature of their married life.

On most days, they would start squabbling soon after they woke up. Over time, Amal's voice became less like thunder bolts. Dotage also blunted the sharpness of his verbal missiles. Like a veteran warrior, Kalyani would capitalize on her opponent's weaknesses and end up cornering him.

For the last two days, Amal, down with a fever, had been confined to bed. He had a feeling that Lord Yama, the God of Death, was about to throw the noose around his neck. Even though he was unable to move, his mind was racing around trying to figure out how to ensure that his wife would never get the key to the safe where the money was kept. He ignored the truth that one cannot take anything when life ends.

An Ongoing Drama

Though his condition was deplorable, Amal continued barking like a toothless dog at Kalyani, who seethed with resentment. She was like a slave awaiting the death of her master.

One twilight, Lord Yama trussed Amal up and hauled him away kicking and screaming. Amal did not want to give up his wealth, but time respects none. Everyone, from a red ant to a blue whale, must surrender to the Grim Reaper.

When the hero exited the stage, the heroine started wailing like a banshee: "O God, you've left me high and dry! Why didn't you take me also?"

Hearing Kalyani's cries, the Lord of Death and his assistants laughed. They knew that if they had invited her to come along with them, she would have refused stoutly. Not only that, she would most likely have asked them to extend her lifespan.

After a while, Kalyani became weary of her own histrionics. She looked out of the window and thought, "It's not night yet. Time sure seems to be crawling. My stomach is growling with hunger. All that crying has made my throat dry. Can't these neighbors bring me some tea at least? Or are they here just to gawk at me and gossip?

"I might have overdone the crying. Anyway, I'm exhausted now. My husband is dead and gone; there's nothing anybody can do about it. I wish I could lie down for a while. But what if I doze off and start snoring? Even before my husband died, the neighbors used to make snide remarks about our bickering. Oh, I just wish this funeral ceremony will get over soon. I hope I don't fall sick."

As Kalyani let her thoughts run amok, a few men carried Amal's corpse to the burial site. There was a peal of thunder followed by flashes of lightning. There would be heavy rains tonight.

After the funeral ceremony, when the visitors had left, a hush fell over the house. Kalyani's mind also started to settle down. The emotions that had been agitating the inner lake of her mind subsided and she began to reflect. "Even though we encounter death, why is it that we don't think that it will claim us also one day? Isn't it the height of foolishness to think we are immortal? Amal struggled and schemed for the sake of money but left empty-handed. I, too, am tired of running after momentary pleasures. Shouldn't I turn to the path of truthfulness, at least now, even though it's a little late?" As the night progressed, such truths began to surge in the widow's heart.

Later, she came into possession of the safe, which Amal's soul had not been able to take with him. Watching her clutching a bunch of keys tightly, we might laugh at Kalyani for trying to cling to the transient pleasures of the world. But let us not forget that many of us are like her and that our names are also in Lord Yama's list.

Moral of the Story:

An awareness of death encourages us to adhere to values. Life is edging ever closer towards death, which is like a period at the end of a sentence. Life will begin again, like a new sentence.

We live as if hypnotized by the world. When we encounter the death of a loved one, we feel sad and express regret. But we shut our eyes to the fact that sooner or later, death will claim us as well.

The fabric of life is woven with the warp and weft of joys and sorrows. Instead of being tossed about by the waves of opposing emotions, the purpose of life is to swim across to the shore of immortality so that we can enjoy everlasting bliss.

An Ongoing Drama

It is not enough to think only about life; shouldn't we also contemplate the inevitability of death? Only through such inquiry can the mind gain maturity. ❀

"True progress is broadening the mind and making the heart expansive. Amma is not saying that external gains or progress is unnecessary; they certainly are. The lofty culture of ancient India gave prime importance to values. Only if we become rooted in this culture can we make real outer and inner progress."

—Amma

Lament of the Jasmines

Though the month of *Makara* (from mid-January to mid-February) was chilly, Neeraj got up early to bathe and felt energized after his bath. He brushed his unruly hair, which was tinted with various shades of brown.

"Hello Neeraj!" his mother called out. "Aren't you going to the temple? It's your birthday!"

At these words, Neeraj shuddered momentarily and even forgot the song he had been humming. His mother continued, "If you want to prosper, you must pray to the family deity and invoke his blessings."

As he walked, Neeraj began to reminisce. For as long as he could remember, he had frequented the area that led to homes with hallowed names such as Ramvihar, Srimandiram, Shivam and Layam, the names also being those of well-known families. These homes used to be hubbubs of festive activity. But now, there was only silence within them. Even the pathways to their homes had become dilapidated.

One of the family members said, "Our elders, who were slaves to wealth and power, brought about this decline of our joint family traditions."

The self-styled oracles of the old generation were stirred by this talk of deteriorating values. But the women of the house ignored them and continued to adorn the living room with the trappings of modernity. In spite of all their efforts, they could not ignore the sense of disintegration gnawing away at them.

Fragments of the past would revisit Neeraj from time to time, like an unexpected fog. He had spent his childhood with his grandmother. On most days, he used to accompany her to the temple. These visits to the temple were not strictly for religious purposes; his grandmother was not above using the occasions to flaunt her social prestige.

Grandma Vishalakshi of Layam and Devaki-amma of Shivam had been strong critics of Neeraj's grandmother. Despite that, whenever they saw Neeraj, they would speak to him affectionately. Even when they were well past 60 years old, they were still well-groomed. These dames radiated an air of aristocracy, prestige and even auspiciousness. What about the people today? They seem to lack that distinction.

When Neeraj reached the Sadashiva Perumal Temple, he was roused from his reveries. Was it the same temple he used to visit, he wondered? This anxiety made him restless. The memories that flooded his mind took him back to his childhood days.

Years ago, not satisfied with offering a moonbeam flower at the shrine, Neeraj had also plucked a hibiscus. His mother had objected. "A hibiscus for Lord Shiva?" In those days, people were sticklers for tradition.

Halfway through his walk to the temple, Neeraj had noticed that flowers from the jasmine shrub at the edge of his teacher's garden had fallen and drifted outside, where they carpeted the road and gave out a sweet fragrance. Resisting the temptation to pick up the fallen flowers, Neeraj plucked a few from the shrub instead.

That was when the flowers on the road began to lament. "Though we're from the same tree, you did not choose us to be offered at the holy feet of the Lord. It's not only you, no one cares about us. People want only the flowers from the shrub. Is it our lot to be treaded upon and ignored? Such discrimination! We are from the same tree and exude the same fragrance, but you don't see that. Why do you not have equal vision? Who instilled in you these erroneous notions of 'pure and impure' and 'high and low?'"

The jasmine plant had been nourished by water and fertilizer. The loving hands of the gardener who nourished it had removed the plant's fear of humans and made it a happy shrub. But hearing the heartbroken lamentations of the fallen flowers hurt it. Slowly, it started shedding its sprigs. Its leaves shriveled and fell to the ground. Distress turned into disease.

In the meantime, as was customary in Kerala, Neeraj removed his shirt before entering the temple. He rang the bell that hung outside the shrine. Hearing it, the priest came out and gave Neeraj the milk-and-banana *prasad* (consecrated food) that had been offered to the Lord at dawn.

He noticed now that the temple premises had undergone a complete facelift. He had never imagined that even a sacred space would change in the name of modernity.

Seeing the stunned look on his face, the priest chuckled. Had they revamped the shrine also? It was the earthly abode of the Lord and the subordinate deities. Neeraj felt disturbed when he thought about how people could disregard tradition in the name of a renovation that seemed only to make things uglier.

To quieten his mind, Neeraj stood with palms joined in prayer, silently expressing his deep reverence and devotion to the Lord.

Moral of the Story:

Time inevitably brings about change. Aren't we constantly changing from cradle to grave? Instead of resisting the riverine flow of time, we should let it take us further ahead. Growth is desirable.

However, we should reflect on this deeply. Not all growth is a sign of progress. Obesity, for example, is a form of expansion but not a sign of good health.

In ordinary life, progress often follows a pattern of leaping forward and a frantic plummeting, whereas in spiritual life, it leads to the realization of the Self. Spirituality takes us inward towards the soul. It makes our heart more expansive.

We all seek to fulfill ourselves, but do not consider if the actions we perform to fulfill our aspirations are in harmony with natural law. If we desire peace in the mind and in the universe, we must first silence the mind. In this way, we can revitalize ourselves internally.

Endless are the glories of nature, which are the manifest forms of God. One who seeks Him, who created these glories by mere will, begins the journey to self-fulfillment. Once we realize that we are one with God, the very epitome of perfection, our growth becomes complete. ❁

"He who is goal-oriented will not postpone his duties. Why procrastinate, knowing that lost time can never be recovered? He who uses his time wisely is intelligent. If we live with total awareness in the present moment, we will never ever have cause for regret later."

—Amma

The Voice of Conscience

"'Let's not do it today. We can do it tomorrow.' I've never thought like this before." The mirror continued, "The day I stop reflecting, I'll stop being myself and become just a piece of glass. Reflection is my duty. I do my duty constantly, the way the heart continues beating. But why are you like this? You spend hours in front of me. In case you're wondering why I'm asking, it's because you treat me in one way as your conscience."

He had been wiping his face before the mirror. When he heard the voice, he started trembling. The voice of his reflection... wasn't it the inner voice of his conscience?

His mind went back two weeks. As usual, it had been a busy morning. His mother and wife were in the kitchen, busily preparing food for him and the children, who were getting ready at a snail's pace. He was still in front of the mirror, dyeing the white streaks of his hair and trying to keep old age at bay.

Suddenly, he noticed his mother standing behind him in the mirror. She said, "It has been two days since Uncle was admitted into the hospital. Have you gone to see him even once?"

He only remembered it when his mother mentioned it. But he said, "Both of you are going to see him daily. Isn't that enough?

Neither of you has any other commitment. So, you can't understand my difficulties. I'll go and see him later."

He could see his mother's face more clearly than his own. She started talking about the past again. "After your father died, Uncle took care of you. He ensured that you received a good education. That was how you got such a good job. But now you say that you don't have time to go and see him. You should remember that he is also your father-in-law. Isn't it your responsibility to take care of your parents-in-law? Even yesterday, Uncle said that he hasn't see you for a long time. He is an elderly man. What's the use of saying 'Later?' What if something untoward happens? There would be no point regretting things later, would there?"

Feeling irritated, he raised his voice and repeated that he had little time.

As he stood before the mirror now, he recalled the conversation with his mother from two weeks ago. As he stood there in silence, he saw his mother and wife coming up behind him. Their tear-filled eyes were glinting with anger that could have reduced him to ash. Uncle had passed on, unable to see his son-in-law, who had always procrastinated. What was the use of talking about it now?

As if to rub salt into his wound, the mirror continued, "You've never shown the enthusiasm you have for your work for anything else. It's not that you lack the time; what you lack is sincerity. You never forget to eat or sleep. You never stop doing anything you like. Have you ever stopped dyeing your hair? Think about it: you give your hair more importance and affection than you gave your uncle!"

He started reflecting. The body perishes just as a river dries up. When we encounter death around us, we don't realize that we will also die one day. The vulture of death can tear our body apart any time. To get caught up in the rat race without giving even a thought to death is foolish. Isn't nature constantly hinting about the inevitability of death through the passing of time, from dawn to dusk, and the passing of seasons, from spring to winter? Just as water evaporates imperceptibly, life is ebbing away slowly from the body.

He wondered, why did I not even try to repay all that Uncle did for me? Who defeated me? Uncle or time?

"You defeated yourself," said the mirror.

As the words of the mirror reverberated in his heart, he made a firm decision that he would never again give excuses and would move in harmony with time. For a moment, he stood focusing all his attention inwards. Then he fell prostrate; it was a prostration to the Lord of Time.

Moral of the Story:

When we put off doing our duties and tasks that time assigns us, we are failing ourselves by a lack of sincerity. To procrastinate in the name of attending to other tasks is a lame excuse. By doing so, we are turning our back on our duties and responsibilities. Time is not in our hands or under our control. That being the case, how can we be so sure that there will be a 'tomorrow' or a 'later' to do those tasks we have postponed?

The wheel of time will continue rolling, whether or not we attend to the task at hand. Time waits for no man. If we don't use our time sensibly, we are squandering a precious gift. Foolish is he who wastes time, and wise is he who recognizes the value of time and uses it properly. ❁

"Children, no one has ever become totally sated by worldly pleasures. The more we indulge, the more we will crave. There is no end to either desires or waves in the ocean. We cannot live without desire. However, only if we exercise control over our desires can we understand what true inner bliss is. A mind without desire is divine in nature."

—Amma

Countless Sea Waves

"Dad, I'm scared of the dark! Please do not let the sun set today," whimpered the girl.

As she watched the bright red sun sink into the ocean, she cried, thinking that her father could stop the sun. "Oh no, it's going to sink! Catch the sun, dad! I want to see it!"

At first, the father laughed. Later, he felt that he must enlighten his daughter.

Actually, quite a few of those who came to the beach had chuckled, hearing the girl's outburst. Behind their smiles was the knowledge that a sunrise always brings a sunset, a morning means an evening, and birth implies an inevitable death. One who knows the ineluctable laws of Mother Nature will be amused when they hear someone protest her ways. Those who know the truth look on sympathetically at those who bawl when their dreams are shattered. When cries follow laughter, isn't the creator of cosmic laws trying to tell us that the flowers of happiness always come with the thorns of sorrow?

The father tried to console his distressed daughter. As soon as he showed her a piece of candy, she stopped crying instantly. Her father showed her four or five candies that looked like bright, orange suns. Those eyes, which had been filled with tears, started sparkling with happiness. The father, a businessman, congratulated himself for successfully winning over his daughter, as if this were yet another business deal he had clinched.

In a sense, isn't the mind a first-rate businessman? It suavely sells us material pleasures and persuades us to attach our senses to them, with the promise of sensory satisfaction.

The delighted daughter was counting the candies: "One, two, three..." In her glee, she did not notice that the sun had set. Having pacified his daughter, the father started drawing figures on the sand; he was trying to tally expenses and revenue, and realized that no matter how much the revenue went up, expenses would increase proportionately. Why, he wondered?

While thus absorbed in calculations, his daughter tapped him and asked, "Dad, will the waves ever subside once and for all?" He simply said no so that he could continue with his calculations. The daughter then starting counting the waves lashing the shore. But when the count began exceeding her counting abilities, she stopped.

Human beings toil hard to fulfill the endless waves of desire that buffet the shores of the mind. In so doing, we lose all peace of mind. It doesn't matter what we study. Unless we practice awareness, we can never know peace.

Neither daughter nor father wanted to leave the beach even though it was now dark. Birds were returning to their nests. It was time for them to return home too. He thought, "What's there to enjoy there? The faces of everyone at home are clouded by dissatisfaction. Their words are either accusations or boasts. No one seems to have time for anything else."

One who is busy does not engage in Self-inquiry. They don't even know about what to inquire. What is the point of existence when we are so caught up in the world that we forget the search for our own Self?

Years ago, he, too, had been building castles in the air: home, wife, child... Even though he had fulfilled all his aspirations, the only thing he felt was an undeniable dissatisfaction.

When he told his daughter that it was time to go home, she said no. When he picked her up, she started crying and pointing to the sea. After walking some distance, they reached his motorbike. She was still crying when he placed her on the bike. When he sternly told her to stop crying, she did not. To prevent the nippy air from getting inside her ears, he covered her head with a scarf. Vexed, she wrenched it away and cried, "I don't want to go home. I want to stay here!"

As he started his bike, the man thought about how trying it would be to ride a bike in the cold wind with a crying child for a pillion. For ages, he had been thinking about buying a car but nothing had materialized. As he rode, he felt the burden of unfulfilled desires and dissatisfaction.

It was after several years of similar longing that he had come in possession of this bike. In those days, he had considered his bike a prized possession. Riding on it, he used to feel as if he had conquered the world.

Moral of the Story:

The longing to possess something fades away the moment we possess it. Whatever we gain sooner or later goes down the trash-can of dissatisfaction. Not realizing this, we continue trying to find happiness in worldly objects. As a result, our sense of dissatisfaction lingers.

Weakness is pursuing material objects for happiness; strength is not being dependent upon them.

If only we could pause our relentless external search and reflect, "Whatever is mine always creates problems whereas the 'I' is never a problem. If all that is 'mine' is removed from 'me,' the only thing that will remain is pure consciousness—the 'I.'" This marks the culmination of Self-inquiry.

Happiness, delight and satisfaction are all to be found within one's own self. The quest for truth is a return journey to the inner realm of bliss. It is like darkness, which can never survive brightness. Similarly, the individual life force can never evade the cosmic life force. Sooner or later, the former will become one with the latter. The sooner the reunion takes place, the better, for it is a return to one's own true self.

One whose mind is riddled with desires can never serve others selflessly; only one without vested interests can. If we work with expectation, we will inevitably be disappointed. Our work should not increase our desires, but decrease them. *Mahatmas* (spiritually illumined souls), who know *dharma* (righteousness), show us the way through example; they are our role models. Neither praise nor censure affects them.

Life is short. Do we want to spend it selfishly? Or should we love and serve others selflessly, and thus make life meaningful? We are free to choose. The wise one chooses the path of peace, and thus lives in a way that benefits both them and the world. ❀

"A mind that is riddled with likes, dislikes and selfishness is like a lake covered with scum. If we can channel the water to a river, the water in the lake will not be stagnant any more. A river, which is ever flowing, does not have the limitations of a lake. An ignorant mind is like a lake, whereas an egoless heart is like a river."

—Amma

A Life that Spreads Fragrance

My name is Sakshi. I live in the peepul tree located on the temple grounds. It's true that, with my tiny wings and small nest, my life during the last rainy season has been a struggle. I can't do much about it either.

"Please give me the strength to spread my tiny wings and fly upwards without falling. Please protect me." This is my prayer and it protects me always.

Once, that noble man who occasionally appears below my nest said, "I was able to tide over disasters by praying for protection and the strength to fly upwards always. We should never lose our poise, either in happiness or sorrow. A mature individual uses the experiences of sorrow to tap into happiness. An ideal devotee is one who accepts both joy and sorrow as gifts from God."

Almost without my knowing, I started yearning for his company, as he was always in a state of bliss. I overcame the natural fear that birds have for humans and moved slowly towards him. I was rewarded with a smile and some fruit from him. He named me Sakshi. Such was the divine power in his voice that by calling out my name just once, I flew straight into his hands and affectionately rubbed my beak against them.

The peepul tree and I would look on with admiration as this holy soul became immersed in meditation under the tree at night. When the sun started to rise, he and I would travel towards the mountain peak to sit still amidst the enchanting beauty of nature.

Once, midway through the journey, he asked, "Are you observing the surroundings? Look around with total attention. Feel the coolness of the lush greenery, gaze at the vast blue sky, and marvel at the golden rays of the early morning sun. Enjoy all these as much as possible. Reflect upon how beautifully the creator of the universe has made this world. It's amazing, isn't it?

"Only when we notice how artistically woven a cobweb is, will we remember the spider that spun it. Sadly, though we see natural marvels all around us, most of us don't recall the divine creator."

We continued sitting on the mountain peak until we began to feel the heat of the sun's rays. The noble man would then disappear as suddenly as he had appeared! We would then have to wait several days for him to reappear.

Over time, the fragrance of the incense, the decoration of lights, and the sounds of mantra chanting issuing from the temple shrine inspired devotion to the Supreme in the peepul and me. Often, a few devotees would come to the peepul tree after their prayers. Unfortunately, they would spend their time there gossiping.

Does one become a devotee merely by smearing sacred ash on one's forehead? Is standing before the shrine and crying out to the Lord an act of devotion? How can it be, when the same person engages in violent acts later? What's the point of criticizing them? They know no better. The fact is, there is no need to make a show of devotion if our hearts are brimming with love for God.

In the absence of that divine soul, the platform around the peepul would be assaulted by the cacophonous voices of the gossip mongers, and stained by decaying leaves from the peepul and the droppings of birds like me. At least our droppings would drive away the gossipers, but only temporarily. They would return the next day to continue blabbering. They even slandered the innocent, noble soul.

Four or five days ago, the scandal mongers shifted the base of their operations to the river side, much to my and the peepul tree's relief. What drove them away was the unbearable stench coming from an open hole, which had been dug in the temple grounds for some purpose and which had since become filled with rainwater and slush. This water had stagnated, leading to the breeding of mosquitos. Regular visitors to the temple would take another route to the temple; others would pinch their noses as they walked past. Some would even comment, "What a foul smell! Isn't there anyone to clean this place?"

They forget that keeping the environment clean and litter-free is everyone's responsibility. Although the temple authorities were aware of the stagnant water, no one was willing to clear it. Instead, they accused each other of neglecting their duties. They continued going past the stinking hole without doing anything about it.

One morning, we saw the saintly man working at the stink-hole. His presence gladdened our hearts. Onlookers made various remarks. One said, "At least, he took the initiative to clean it up!" Another said, "He doesn't have any work to do. Let him do this at least. Such people ought to engage in selfless service."

The man ignored all such remarks and engaged himself in the work of draining the hole of the slimy water. Then, he cleaned himself and sat down below the peepul tree. He spoke to me and the peepul tree. As he spoke, compassion was overflowing from his eyes. "Anything that flows is liquid. Stagnant water is also liquid. Although both are the same, what a stark contrast there is between them! One is clean whereas the other is slimy. It is like the difference between the pure self and the living soul. It is the duty of the wise to lead the ignorant ones, who have stagnated in the slime of materialism, to the realm of the Self. The wise ought to become the light of knowledge for those stumbling in the darkness of ignorance. But if they are not interested in the truth, no one can save them."

Smiling, the noble one continued, "Actually, the stench was from the impure minds of people here. One can only express what is inside him or her, whether good or bad. There is nothing outside that is not an expression of what is inside. Hence, isn't this universe one's own creation?

"Blaming others for problems is foolishness. Instead, one must correct one's mistakes and try to rise above one's limitations, and in this way, move ahead. By focusing on the drawbacks of others, we are straying away from purity. By engaging in self-introspection, we gravitate towards purity and God.

"It's not body consciousness that we should cultivate but self-awareness; or, awareness of the Almighty."

Hearing these words, my heart was filled with the light of inspiration. The leaves of the peepul tree began to flutter. Both of us were eager to attain self-fulfillment through divine grace.

Moral of the Story:

He who whiles away his time in gossip will be killed by the noose of time, whereas he who heeds the words of the wise will cross the ocean of life and reach the shore of immortality.

A mind that is in the grip of likes, dislikes and selfishness is like a lake covered by scum. If we can connect the lake water to a river, the water in the lake will not become stagnant. A grand river that is ever flowing is not like a lake, which is constrained. An ignorant mind is like a stagnant lake, whereas a mind devoid of the ego is like a river. ❀

A mind in the grip of likes, dislikes and selfishness is like a lake covered by scum. If we can connect the lake water to a river, the water in the lake will not become stagnant. A grand river that is ever flowing is not like a lake, which is constrained. An ignorant mind is like a stagnant lake, whereas a mind devoid of the ego is like a river."

—Amma

Bliss of Union

For several days, seeing the river flowing below, a block of ice in a snowy mountain had a doubt: where was the river going? Finally, it asked the river itself this question: "Where are you headed? Why are you constantly flowing away, leaving the mountain? Can't you stay still in one place, like me?"

The river gurgled in laughter. Hearing this, the ice block became angry, thinking that the river was mocking him. In the heat of anger, the ice block started melting, becoming separated from the mountain, and fell into the river. It started bawling. "O river, please don't take me away. I don't want to leave the mountain. I'd much rather stay here."

The river replied sweetly, "Why fear? Aren't we both made of the same stuff? Look at me: I'm not leaving the mountain and going anywhere. I'm always in my heart, even as I flow into the ocean."

With its blue eyes that matched the color of the sky, the river smiled at the ice block, who wondered how someone could be both the origin and the destination... and everywhere!

The river added, "What's the use of having knowledge? Only when it becomes an experience does true understanding dawn. You can find me in the flow. Come with me. Don't be frightened."

Bliss of Union

The ice block said, "Although I wish to know more about you, I have no desire to leave the mountain to gain that knowledge."

With utmost affection, the river said, "Dear child, don't be frightened. You may feel that you're losing something, but you're not. You'll come to realize this at the end. Be brave and flow with me."

The ice block started flowing with the river. Initially, it was scared as the river flowed downward, and it closed its eyes. When it opened its eyes slowly, it was amazed by what it saw. All around were colors it had never seen in its life. The river acknowledged its amazement with a gentle smile and said, "This is known as riverside beauty. From here, you can see the greenery of the forest and the beauty of the flowers."

A few flowers that had fallen into the river touched the ice block, which became entranced by their sweet fragrance. When a breeze blew and threatened to take the flowers away, the ice block anxiously tried to cling to the flowers by swimming against the current. Seeing this, the river reprimanded the ice block: "No! Don't go against the flow. That's foolish! You didn't come in search of flowers. Enjoy whatever comes your way but forget about it when it passes. There's no point in celebrating or grieving over what comes and goes."

Though the ice block continued to go with the flow, the thought of the flowers made its heart heavy. The river affectionately reminded it, "Didn't I tell you at the start of our journey that you won't lose anything? Then why be sad? This sorrow will only obstruct your vision, causing you to miss what you ought to see. Try not to be attached to anything. Just observe and learn from it."

The ice block felt partly reassured by the river's words of assurance, but half its mind was still with the flowers. While it was in this state of inattentiveness, the ice block was sucked into a vortex. As it started rotating at high speed, it began to melt at an even faster rate. Just as the ice block came face to face with the terrifying prospect of disappearing forever, the river lifted it away and saved it from the vortex. Much relieved, the ice block continued flowing.

As it flowed, a new-found respect for the river arose in the ice block's heart. It saw people using the river in different ways: some bathing or swimming in it; others quenching their thirst with its waters; and yet others dumping waste into it. The river caressed them all with gentle love. Its attitude towards those who praised or reviled it was the same. This ice block's respect towards the river transformed into admiration. When it realized that the river nourished all life forms, its reverence surged into devotion.

There is rhythm to the flow of the river. As soon as the ice block became aware of it, its heart began beating to that rhythm. As it became more familiar with the river, the ice block wanted to plumb the depths of the river. In that love, it melted completely, became one with the river, and flowed towards the ocean. It realized that the mountain, river and ocean are all in itself. It began to feel that there was nothing other than itself.

In this realization, it became aware of the low hum of the 'Omkara' (Aum). In that state of non-duality, which is the very substratum of the creation, it was overcome by a rapturous bliss. The ice block understood, "I see myself in you. If I truly see my Self, I see everything."

Moral of the Story:

Unless we know the 'One,' we cannot know everything. Knowledge of the many need not give us knowledge of the 'One.' We must impress this idea on the soul, the source of all wisdom.

Bliss of Union

The Guru's grace guides the spiritual seeker along the path of righteousness. When the heart merges with the holy feet of the Guru, all duality disappears; only oneness remains. ❀

Acknowledgments

My sincere thanks to Br. Madhavamrita Chaitanya and Sri. Madhavan of Palakkad for their help in preparing this manuscript, Sri. Arun Raj for the front and back cover design, and the staff of Amrita Offset Printers for their help in printing this book. ❀

www.ingramcontent.com/pod-product-compliance
Lightning Source LLC
Chambersburg PA
CBHW061957070426
42450CB00011BA/3129